Wolfgang Schnepper

Competitive games in football training for youth and adults

Wolfgang Schnepper, Born 1964, Cetified Sports Teacher
Ex-Bezirksliga player in football,
1988-89 successful german triathlete,
1990 Bayerischer champion in Body-Building,
1998 / 99 Fitness coach in paid football,
2003 - 2006 Physical education teacher at a comprehensive school

Bibliografische Informationen der Deutschen Nationalbibliothek: Die Deutsche Nationalbibliothek verzeichnet diese Publikation in der Deutschen Nationalbibliografie; detaillierte bibliografische Daten sind im Internet über http://dnb.d-nb.de abrufbar.

©2023 Wolfgang Schnepper

Herstellung und Verlag: BoD – Books on Demand, Norderstedt
Satz und Layout: Wolfgang Schnepper

ISBN 978-3-7412-5356-0

Table of contents

Preface..6
Category 1 competitive games.........................7
Category 2 competitive games.......................11
Category 3 competitive games.......................26
Bibliography..41

 # Preface

The best way to learn football is under competitive conditions during training. Here we present many competitive games in training, which, for example, promote tackling and goal-shooting training under real conditions. These competitive games should account for 30 to 50 percent of the total training time. They almost always take place at the end of the training. The last competitive game is usually a normal football game without any special technical or tactical specifications.

The competitive games in this book are divided into three categories:

Category 1 with easy requirements (usually only conditional and/or technical)

Category 2 with medium-difficult requirements (but still practicable from the age of 12)

Category 3 with very difficult and complex requirements (sometimes only usable from 16 years)

Category 1 competitive games

Category 1 competitive games

Category 1 final games can be practiced from the age of 10 at the latest, but make sense up to the senior level.

Left foot

The ball may only be dribbled or kicked with the left foot (headball is of course allowed). This form of play should be limited to 5 to 10 minutes.

Right foot

This time the ball may only be dribbled or kicked with the right foot.

Penalty

The team that concedes a goal must do 5 to 10 push-ups.

Ball Forward

The ball may only be dribbled or kicked forward.

Outnumbered team

One team plays outnumbered for 5 to 10 minutes, then the teams change it.

 # Category 1 competitive games

Variation

One or two soccer players always play for the team that has possession of the ball.

Soccer goal rating

Header goals or particularly good soccer goals count double.

3 corner kicks

3 corner kicks mean a penalty for the corresponding team.

Goalkeeper missing

Each team plays without a permanent goalkeeper.

Football goal made difficult

A soccer goal only counts if all of your own players are above the center line.

1 soccer goal

Only one soccer goal is played.

Category 1 competitive games

Football game on four goals

A football game is played on four goals over 2 x 10 minutes.

Four soccer goals and two balls

Now do the same exercise but with two balls at the same time.

 # Category 1 competitive games

The weight vest

A football game with weight vests may only be used from the age of 16. Each team plays for 5 minutes with a weight vest of 5 to 6 kilograms. If there are not enough vests, they are changed more often.

Goal scorer change

Each team initially plays with the same number of players. The player who scores a goal then immediately changes to the other team. Now it can happen that a team has two or four more players. But then it is so superior that this team will score a goal and then lose a player again, etc.

Special soccer goals

Soccer goals may only be scored with the head, drop kick, after One-two or directly.

Unequal teams

A team is formed with very good players. The other team plays in majority. This form of football game is limited to a maximum of 10 minutes.

Double goalkeeper

Here you play with two goalkeepers on big football goals.

Category 2 competitive games

Category 2 competitive games

Counter attack in soccer

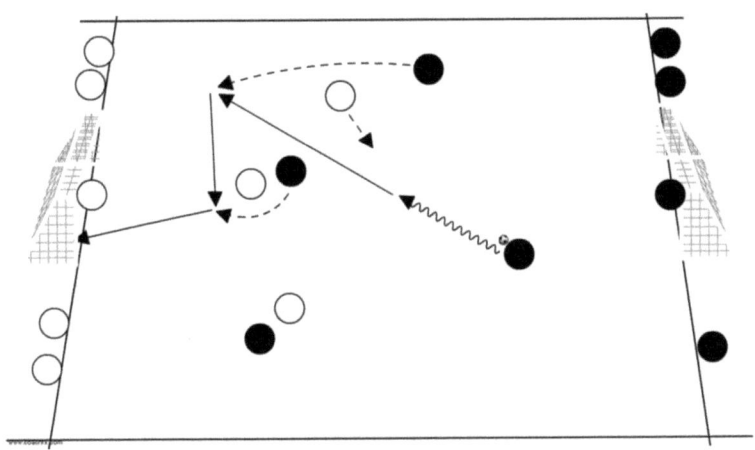

In this described competitive game, we train the fast attack with a majority and the soccer counterattack. The game is played on two occupied goals. The attacking team has four strikers and the defending team has three defenders. The defending team has four players outside the field next to the soccer goal, the attacking team has three players next to their goal (see picture above).

 # Category 2 competitive games

Exercise procedure:

1. The attack must be completed within two minutes, otherwise the strikers have to leave the field and the three waiting players become defenders. The four players who are waiting now become strikers and get the ball, etc. However, each attack is always limited to two minutes.

2. If the defenders get the ball, they must initiate a counterattack immediately and are only allowed to run forward, dribble and shoot. So they are looking for the unconditional goal completion

3. If the soccer strikers finish with a goal, the opponent and his soccer strikers get the ball. Soccer corners and free kicks are executed within the two minutes.

Category 2 competitive games

Soccer game with dribbling action

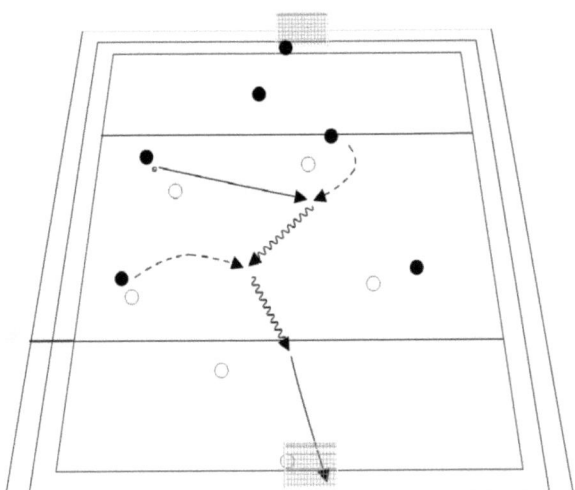

A playing field of 40 x 30 meters is marked. A middle zone of 20 x 30 meters is also marked (see upper picture). Two teams are formed, each with a goalkeeper, one defender each in the defensive zone and 4 to 6 players each in the middle zone.

Procedure: 4 vs 4, 5 vs 5 or 6 vs 6 play in the middle zone. If a player now manages to dribble across the base line in the middle zone towards the opposing goal, he must now look 1 against 1 against the defender to finish the goal. After this action, the other team gets possession of the ball in the middle zone.

 # Category 2 competitive games

Variations:

- The forward calls out the name of a teammate from the middle zone who can assist him in attacking in the opponent's defensive zone.

- Now the defender can also call a player for reinforcements as soon as an striker invades his zone.

- Long-range shots from the center zone are allowed.

- The goalkeeper is allowed to leave the goal line.

- It will be played without a defender.

- 2 to 3 strikers are allowed to enter the defensive zone against a defender and the goalkeeper.

Category 2 competitive games

Just a field of attack

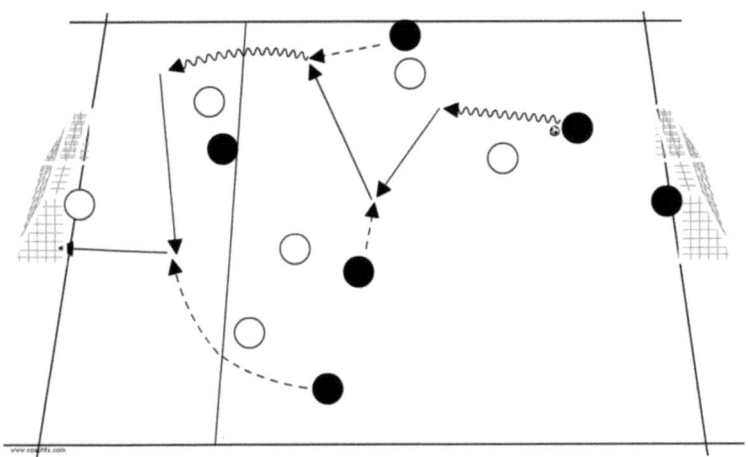

Now only one team has a small attacking field (see picture above)

Procedure: Two teams are formed, each with a goalkeeper. The number of field players is 5 to 7 per team.

A team plays again on the goal with the small attacking field. If this team scores a goal with a long-range shot outside the attacking field, this goal is scored twice, all other goals count once. After ten minutes, the sides of the field are changed.

Category 2 competitive games

Split soccer teams

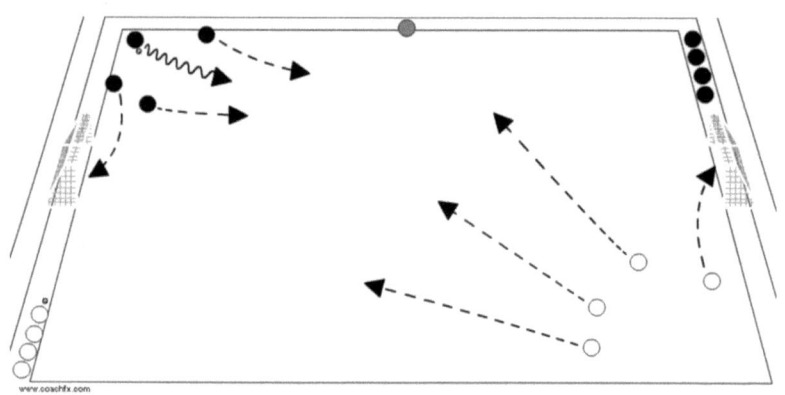

A playing field of about 25 x 20 meters is marked. With 4 vs. 4 to 6 vs. 6 players, the playing field is extended to 30 x 25 meters, etc. Two unoccupied football goals are also available. Each team consists of two groups (four to six players per group). The team parts get the names 1a and 1b and the second team the names 2a and 2b.
They are distributed to the left and right of their own soccer goal (see picture above).

Exercise procedure: The trainer calls up team parts 1a and 2b, for example. These players then run into the playing field and now play against each other, each with a goalkeeper.

 # Category 2 competitive games

At the first call, the ball is in the middle of the field. For example, after two to three minutes the trainer calls out "replace 2b with 2a".
Now team 2b has to leave the field immediately and is replaced by 2a. After another 2 to 3 minutes, the trainer calls out, for example, 1a and 1b and replace 2a with 2b."
So here two parts of the team are exchanged at the same time, etc.

Category 2 competitive games

Only double football goals count

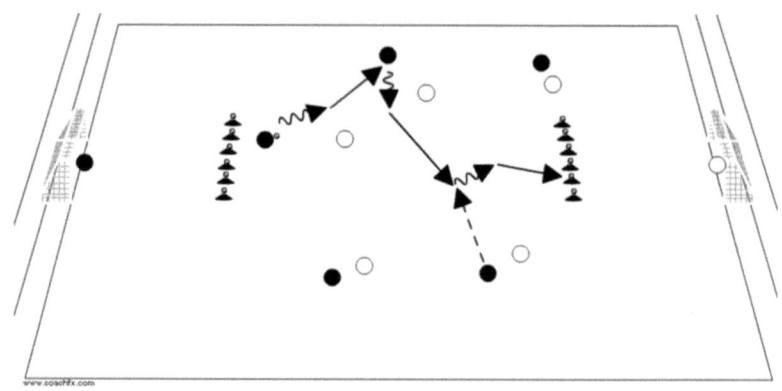

A field of 40 x 25 meters is marked with two football goals. In the playing field, pylons are distributed with a ball on them. Two teams are formed, each with a goalkeeper. Each team consists of 5 to 7 players (look picture above).
Procedure: A normal football game is played, with one difference. Before a team can score a regular goal, a pylon with a ball must first be knocked over by the regular ball. The coach removes the corresponding pylon with the ball from the field.
The corresponding team may now also score a regular football goal. In the meantime, the other team can also shoot down a pylon with a ball and then score a normal soccer goal. If a goal is scored, another pylon must be shot down for the next goal.

# Category 2 competitive games

After all pylons have been shot down, a normal soccer game continues. Overturned pylons must be rebuilt by the player concerned.

Many small football goals in the field

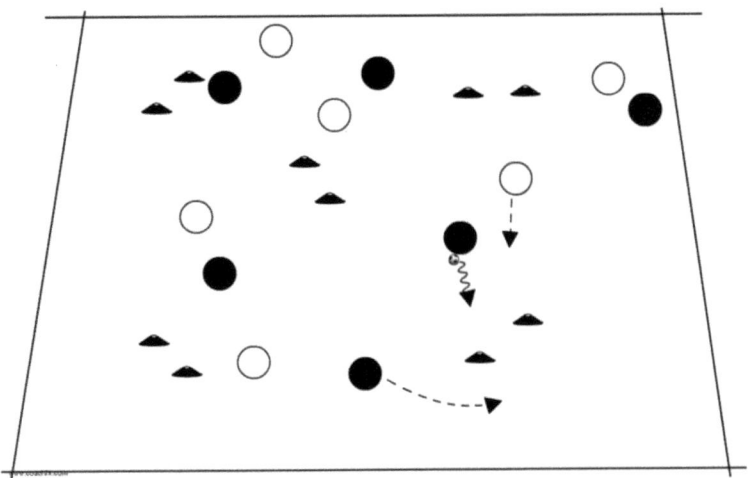

Several small soccer goals are set up with pylons in a small playing field. A minimum of 6v6 is played. The ball shall be played through one of these goals, with a team-mate having to receive the ball from behind the goal for a regular goal to count. The playing time is about 10 minutes.

 **Category 2 competitive games**

Find the team-mate

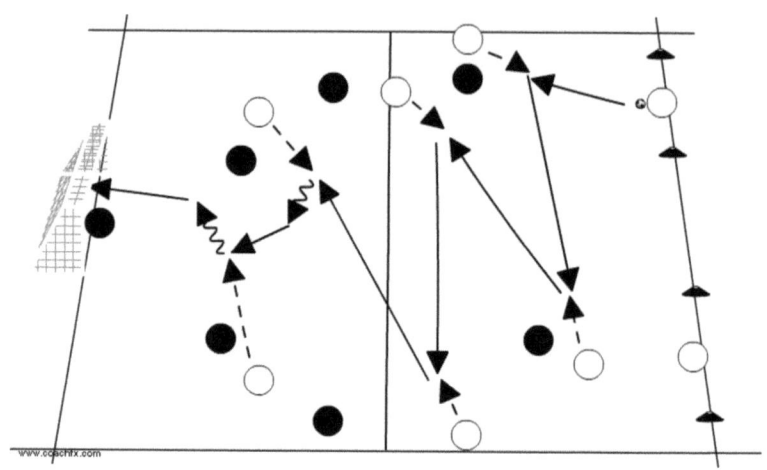

Now a soccer game with 6 to 8 players per team is played on one big soccer goal and two smaller soccer goals. A goalkeeper acts in every soccer goal (see picture above). If a team wins the ball in its own half of the field, it must be played four times in this half of the field before the ball can be played in the opposing half of the field.

Category 2 competitive games

The soccer counter game

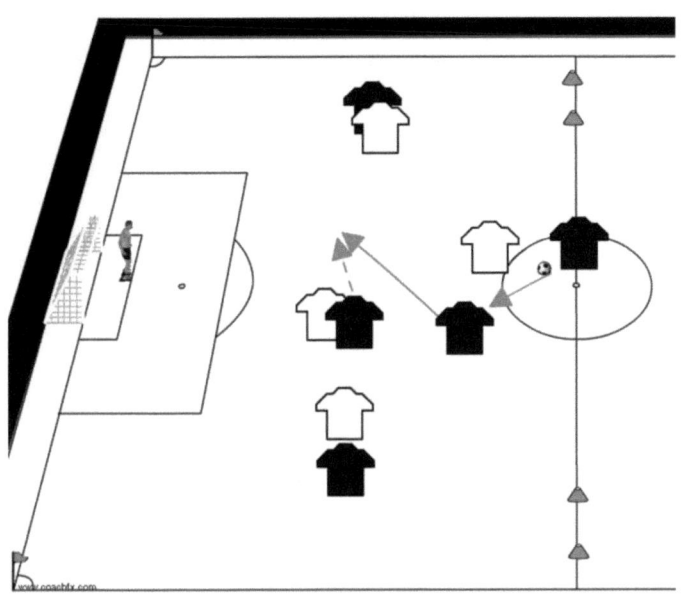

Exercise structure and procedure: We play on half a soccer field (see picture above) 5 against 5, 6 against 5 or 7 against 5. There are two pylon soccer goals on the middle line. The team with the pylon soccer goals should play in the majority and have to look for the goal after 4 to 6 passes. If this is not successful, the other team gets the ball, which plays towards the pylon soccer goals according to the normal rules.

Category 2 competitive games

The soccer counter game 2

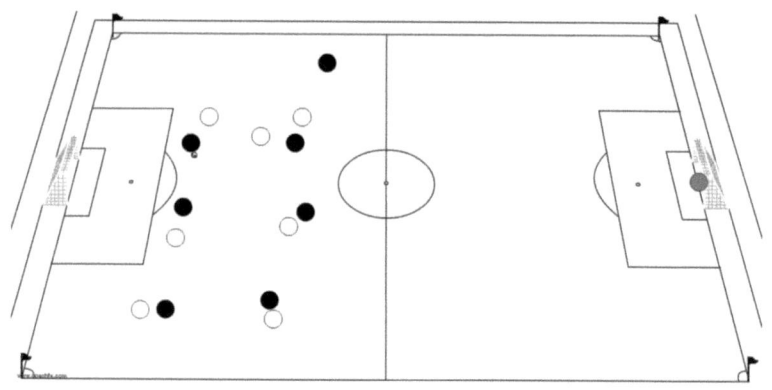

Exercise structure and procedure:

- Entire football field

- Form 2 teams, each with 5 to 7 players

- All players are in a half whose football goal is not occupied.

In this half of football, the two teams play each other without a goal. At the coach's command, the team in possession tries to score a goal in the other half of the football field. There is a goalkeeper in this soccer goal. The other team tries to prevent the goal. Play is now played until one team scores a goal. The game then begins again in the other half of the field.

 # Category 2 competitive games

Team in majority

For example, it is played 7 against 5 on two occupied goals. The team with the majority may only play with three ball contacts. After a few minutes, the other team then plays in majotity, each again with only three ball contacts per person.

Handball Header Volleyball

A 30 x 20 meter soccer field is marked with two occupied soccer goals. Two teams are divided.

Procedure: The ball may only be played with the hands. Soccer goals may only be scored with the head or after a throw with a volley (foot knee or thigh). Header goals count double. Only three steps may be taken with the ball in hand.

I   Play for four goals in the penalty area

t is played for four mini goals in the penalty area. So each team plays for two mini-goals.

Variations: Goals only count after a direct play, ball contacts are limited to three per person, or a neutral player is designated. He always plays for the team in possession.

 # Category 2 competitive games

Play the ball back

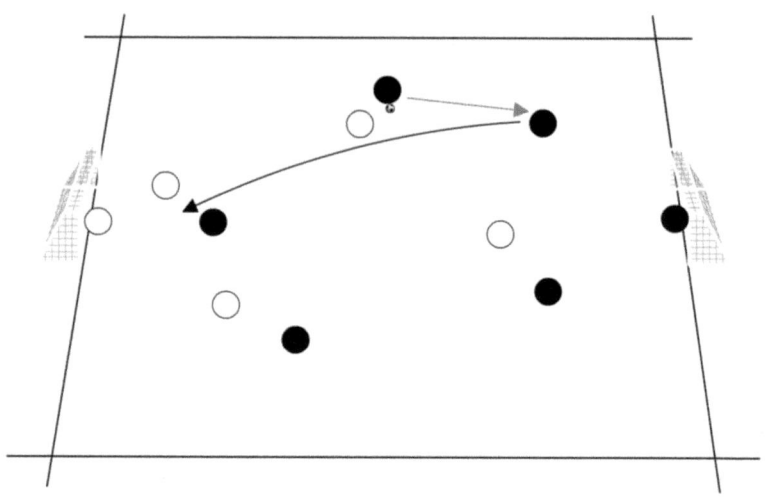

Two teams play against each other on a relatively small field (see picture above). For example, one team has five field players, but the other only four. If the team with the majority wins the ball, it always have to play the ball back first.
The soccer player who now receives the ball must now play the ball directly forward, otherwise there is a free kick for the opponent. We play without offside.

Category 2 competitive games

Additional running training in the football game

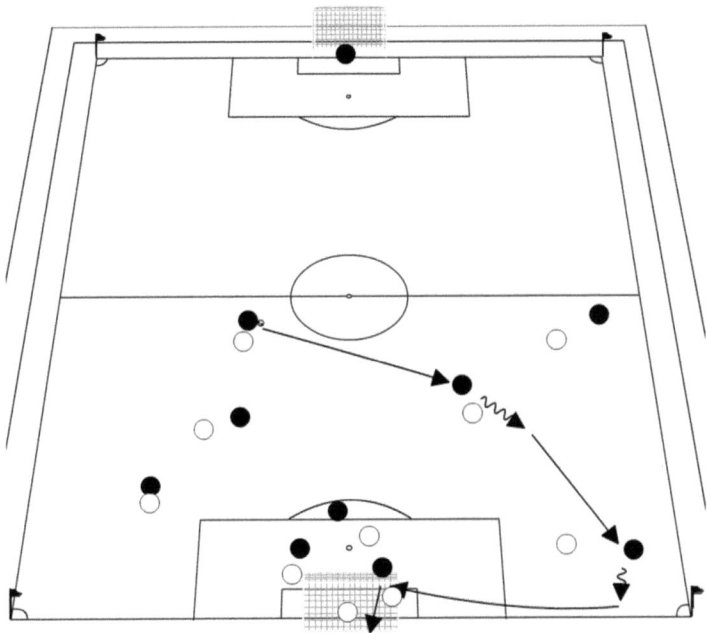

Soccer goals may only be scored if all players of this team are in the opposing half of the game (see picture above).

Category 3 competitive games

Large format soccer table

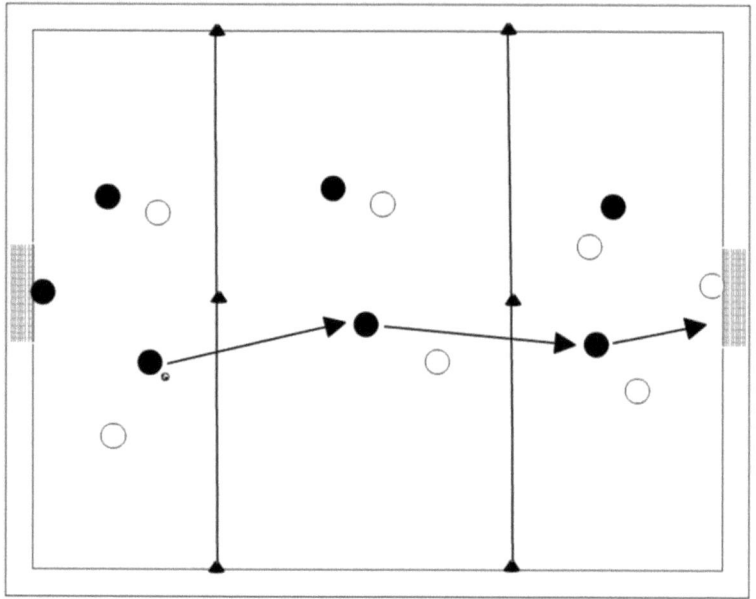

This exercise goes step by step to the highest cognitive, playful and technical demands of soccer players.

Exercise 1: One half of the field with two occupied soccer goals is divided into three fields of equal size (see picture above). For each team, which consists of 7 to 10 players, there is a defensive zone, a midfield zone and an attacking zone. Each zone now has 2 to 3 players per team. In the defensive zone there are then three to four players for the team with the goalkeeper.

 # Category 3 competitive games

The following rules now apply. The players are not allowed to leave their zones, but only shoot the ball into the next zone or the zone after that. The soccer players are also allowed to play back one or two zones.
But players are not allowed to leave their zones. The playing time is five to ten minutes until exercise 2.

Exercise 2: Now a player from the middle zone can be active in all zones, i.e. change zones at will. The playing time is five to ten minutes until the third exercise.

Exercise 3: With one team (but only with one) the entire middle zone may now use the entire playing field. The playing time is 5 minutes.

Exercise 4: One team remains zoning, the other team is free to move. It is played without offside with a playing time of 5 minutes.

Exercise 5: In one team only the midfield may move freely, in the other team all players may move freely. The playing time is 5 to 10 minutes.

Exercise 6: In both teams, only midfield is allowed to move in each zone. The playing time is again 5 to 10 minutes.

Exercise 7: Both teams are again tied to the three zones. However, a team in the midfield zone has two more players. However, this team must play directly in this zone. Playing time is again 5 to 10 minutes.

Category 3 competitive games

Competitive games for switching from defense to attack

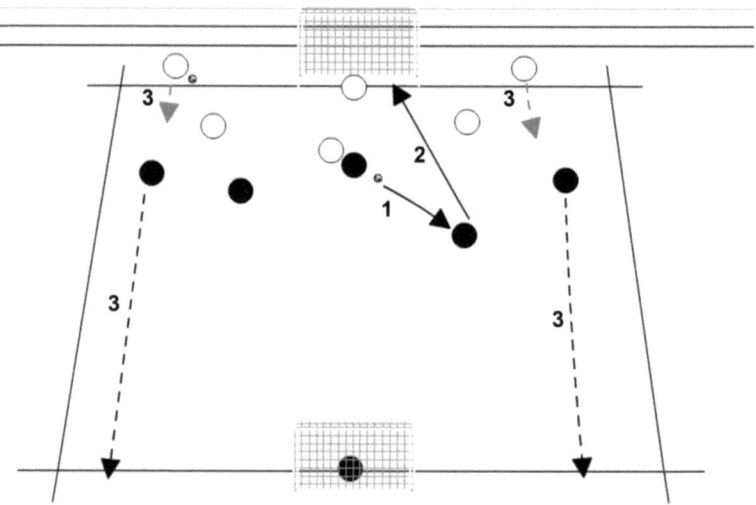

Exercise 1: On a small soccer field with occupied goals, 5 attackers try to score a soccer goal against three defenders (see picture above). There is one player each to the left and right of the defending team's soccer goal. One player has possession of a ball. If the attacking team loses possession, two strikers must leave the field immediately. Now the three defenders become strikers and are immediately supported by the two players next to the soccer goal. These two players become more strikers with their ball and the attack goes to the other soccer goal. The other team's two attackers, who had to leave the field of play, are now also on the left and right of their goal and one of them has possession of the ball. The tasks of attack and defense are constantly changing. Even if a soccer goal is scored, the tasks are changed immediately. Throw-ins and corners are not executed.

 **Category 3 competitive games**

Exercise 2

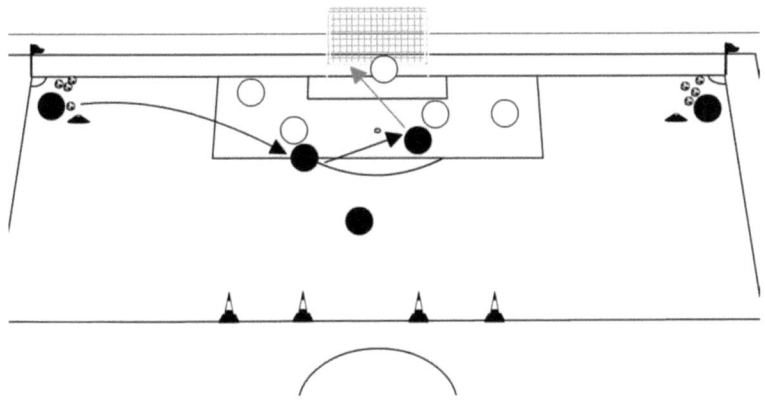

In this exercise, corner kicks are shot into the penalty area alternately from the left and right flanks. The cross balls are made on the run. Two attackers start in the football goal area, which is occupied by four defenders and the goalkeeper, and should use the corner kicks on the goal.
An attacking midfielder lurks behind his strikers, waiting for a possible long-range shot while also securing two small football goals behind him. If the defenders get the ball, they immediately start a counter attack in the direction of the two small soccer goals and try to score a soccer goal. If the attack is successful or not completed, the exercise begins again with the corner kick. The Defenders may only dribble or shoot forward on their counterattack.

Category 3 competitive games

Fire football

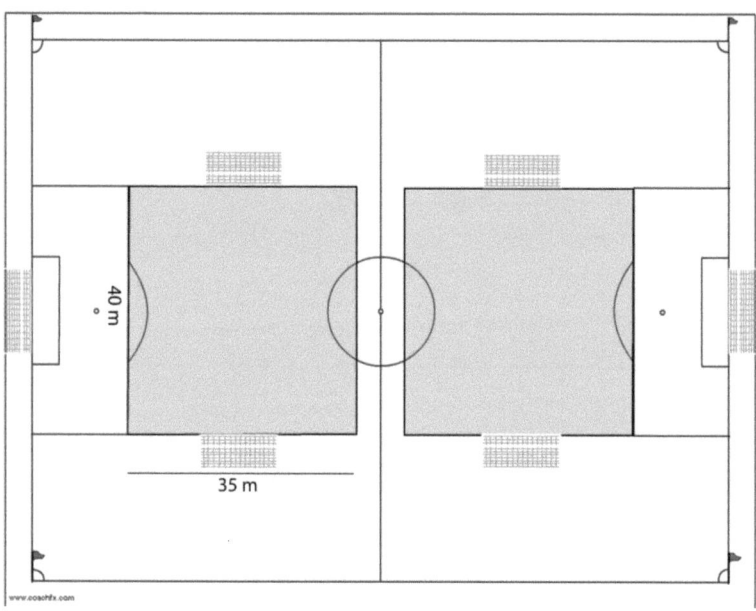

Here we play a 5 against 5 or 6 against 6 on normal football goals with a goalkeeper. However, the playing field is only 40m x 35m (see picture above). As a result, all players are constantly on the move and scoring goals is very common. Corners and throw-ins are not executed. If the ball goes out, the coach of the relevant team throws a new ball at about that point. It is played for about 5 to 10 minutes. After a break of 5 minutes, this form of play can be repeated again. Soccer-specific endurance and goal scoring are optimally trained here.

Category 3 competitive games

Eleven against zero

Now we study moves in football in a progressive sense. We start with an 11 against zero. The team positions itself in the tactical and predetermined basic order on the field. Now an attack and given play is initiated by the goalkeeper and completed by the team. After that, the attack is trained with 11 against 5. The opposing team now consists of a goalkeeper, two defenders and two midfielders.
This is followed by an 11 against 7. The opposing team now consists of a goalkeeper, three defenders, two midfielders and a striker. If the opposing team can fend off the attack and win the ball, play continues until one team scores a goal. Then the team with eleven players repeats the attack and predetermined move.
Finally, an 11 vs 9 is played with the same rules.

Category 3 competitive games

The players move correctly on the soccer field

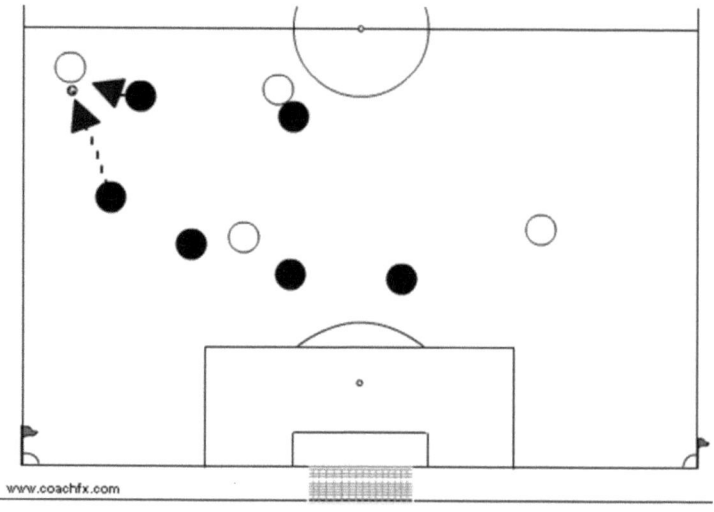

In this competitive game, a team that is in the majority should constantly move and attack the opponent with the ball with two players again and again (see picture above). The playing time is about 10 minutes.

Category 3 competitive games

Long-rang shots

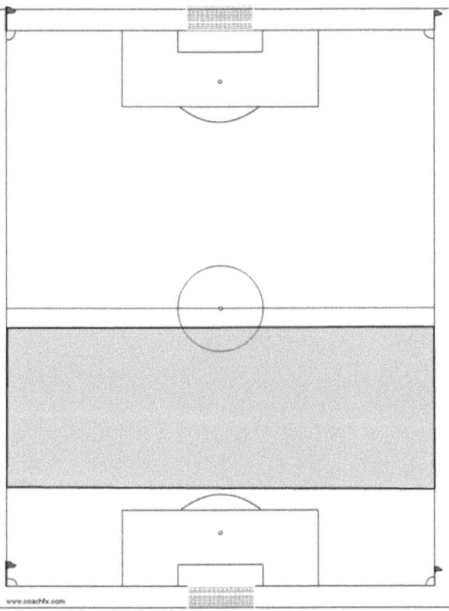

A normal football game is played. However, a team may only score goals from the gray field (see picture above). After 10 minutes the tasks are changed.

 **Category 3 competitive games**

Extreme ball capture

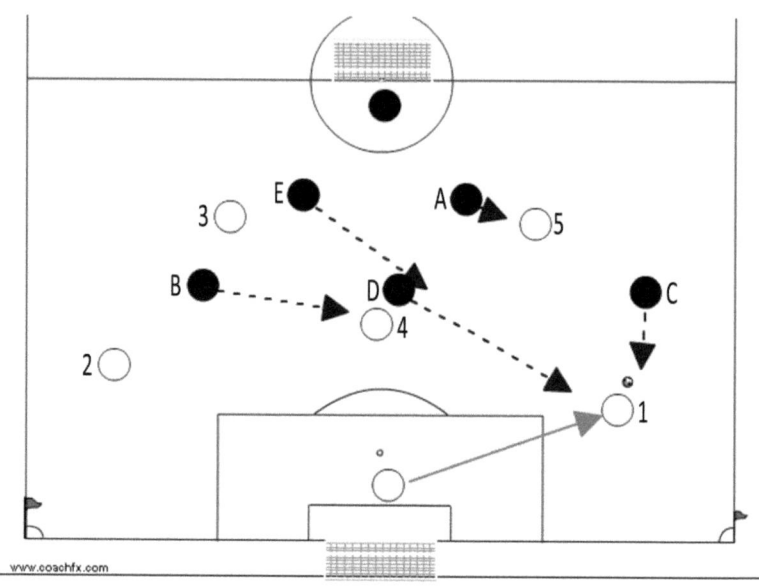

A team plays high risk and tries to win the ball again and again with extreme player extension to the ball-carrying opponent. The playing time is 5 minutes. Then it is the other team's turn.

Category 3 competitive games

All players attack

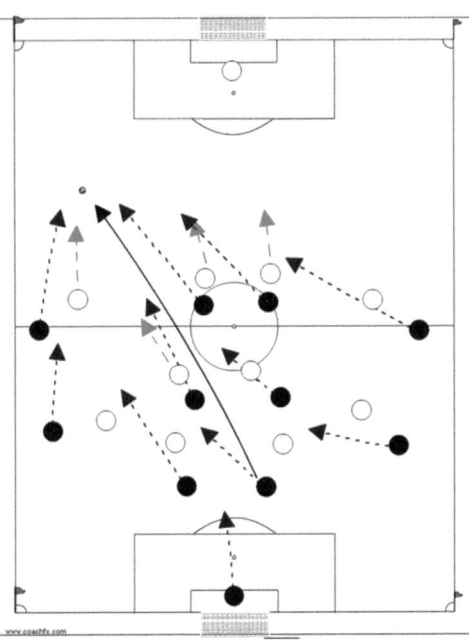

If the ball is won, one of the two teams immediately plays with all players to attack (see picture above). After about 5 to 10 minutes, the other team takes over this task.

# Category 3 competitive games

Triple Attack

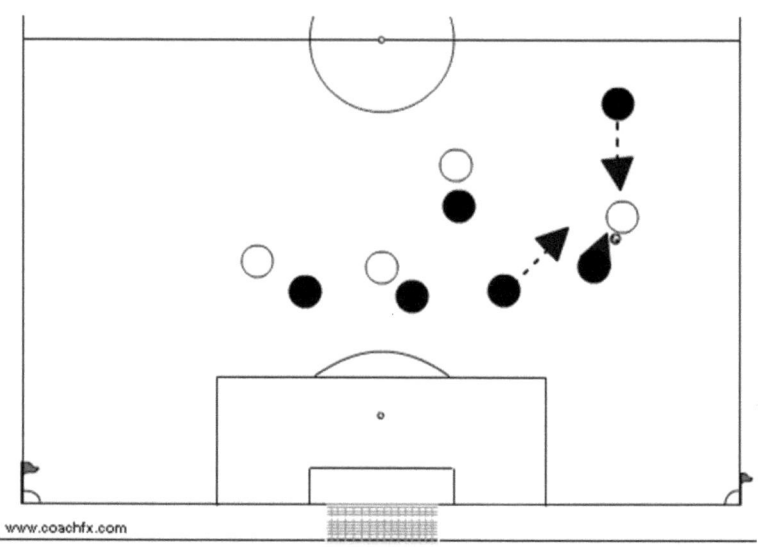

A team should attack the ball-carrying opponent with three players at the same time. After 5 minutes, the tasks are changed.

 # Category 3 competitive games

After losing the ball

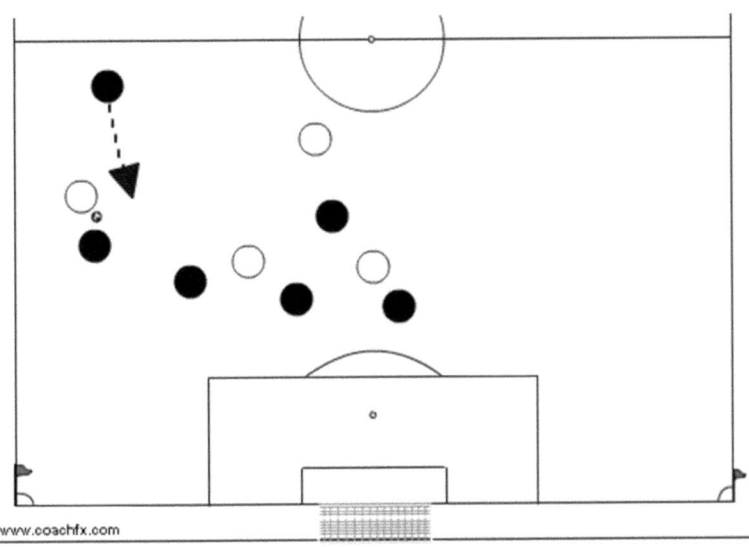

In this competitive game, the strikers of both teams have the task of helping out in defense again and again. So they are in constant motion.

 **Category 3 competitive games**

Anticipate

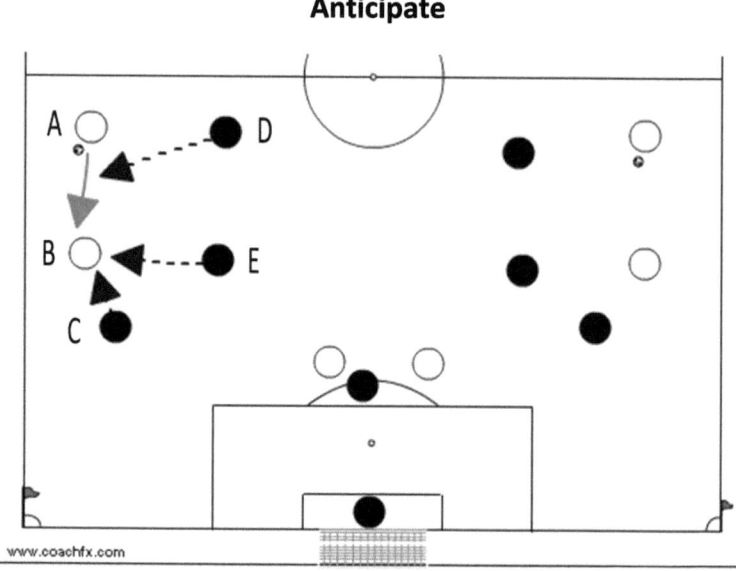

In this soccer training game, the players of both teams have to anticipate who will be played next. That player will then be attacked by two players at once as quickly as possible.

Category 3 competitive games

Direct play in midfield

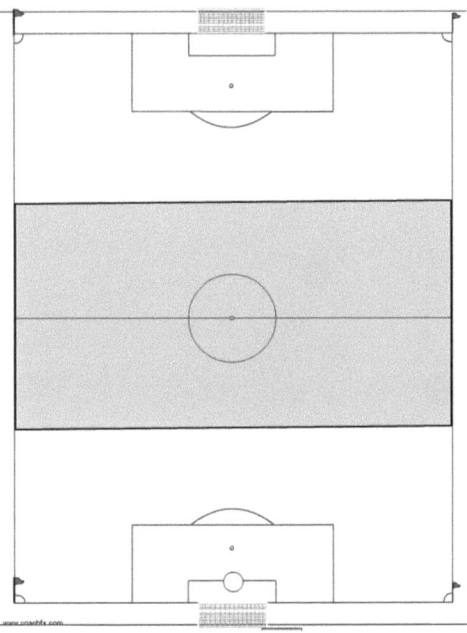

In this football game, the ball may only be played directly in midfield (see picture above).

 # Category 3 competitive games

Extreme Attack

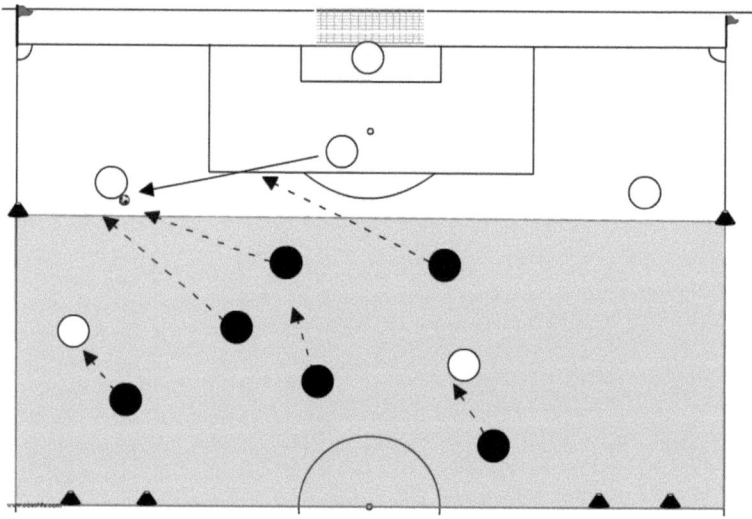

A team is now given the task of attacking immediately (see picture above). The player with the ball is immediately attacked and nearby teammates are man-marked. After 10 minutes the tasks of the teams are changed.

 **Literaturverzeichnis**

Claßen, M. / Schnepper, W.:
Taktiktraining im Jugendfußball, BOD, 2011

Claßen, M. / Schnepper, W.:
Taktiktraining im Jugendfußball 2, BOD, 2012

Claßen, M. / Schnepper, W.:
Pressing mit System, BOD, 2012Claßen, M. / Schnepper, W.:

Schnepper, W. / Claßen, M.
E-Jugend / D-Jugendtraining: effektive Übungen,
BOD, 2014

Schnepper, W. / Claßen, M.
D-Jugend / C-Jugendtraining:
30 komplette Trainingseinheiten,
BOD, 2016

Schnepper, W. / Claßen, M.
D-Jugend / C-Jugend:
über 100 effektive Trainingsübungen
BOD, 2017

 **Notizen**

 **Notizen**

 **Notizen**